# YOUR KNOWLEDGE HAS VALUE

AF136123

- We will publish your bachelor's and
  master's thesis, essays and papers

- Your own eBook and book -
  sold worldwide in all relevant shops

- Earn money with each sale

Upload your text at www.GRIN.com
and publish for free

# Mergers and Acquisitions in Germany. What Are the Specific Requirements For German Medium-Sized Companies?

Felix-Sebastian Ament

**Bibliographic information published by the German National Library:**

The German National Library lists this publication in the National Bibliography; detailed bibliographic data are available on the Internet at http://dnb.dnb.de.

ISBN: 9783346235749
This book is also available as an ebook.

© GRIN Publishing GmbH
Nymphenburger Straße 86
80636 München

Print and binding: Books on Demand GmbH, Norderstedt, Germany
Printed on acid-free paper from responsible sources.

The present work has been carefully prepared. Nevertheless, authors and publishers do not incur liability for the correctness of information, notes, links and advice as well as any printing errors.

GRIN web shop: https://www.grin.com/document/916287

# Assignment – Financial Management

## Requirements for medium-sized Mergers & Acquisitions transactions

What are the specific requirements for Merger & Acquisition transactions in German medium-sized companies?

FOM Hochschule für Oekonomie & Management

## Requirements for medium-sized Mergers & Acquisitions transactions

What are the specific requirements for Merger & Acquisition transactions in German medium-sized companies?

# Table of contents

# List of abbreviations

| | |
|---|---|
| LOI | Letter of Intent |
| R&D | Research and development |
| M&A | Mergers & Acquisitions |
| SME | Small and Medium Enterprise/Small and Mid-sized |
| PMI | Post-Merger Integration |

# List of figures

# 1 Introduction

Digitization and globalization are increasingly forcing German SMEs to compete with foreign companies. New large growth markets outside Germany require an adjustment of the internationalization strategy. To remain competitive, companies must expand existing networks and merge into new networks. Specialize and, if necessary, reduce offers. Increase cost efficiency, optimize and modernize processes and expand production capacities. Furthermore, expand and consolidate the international presence.[1] Rothlauf summarises this as "expansion, diversification, downsizing, outsourcing, and cooperation".[2]

One opportunity to implement these strategies is the implementation of Mergers & Acquisitions. This term is used to describe a merger or fusion of two companies to form a legal and economic unit or the acquisition of company units or an entire company. "M&A stands for all transactions in connection with the transfer and encumbrance of property rights in companies, including the formation of groups of companies, the restructuring of groups of companies, mergers and transformations in the legal sense, squeeze-outs, the financing of the acquisition of companies, the formation of joint ventures and the takeover of companies."[3]

M&A transactions can be achieved through economies of scale and economies of scope by increasing activity within the company. In addition, new internal success potentials can be developed and core capabilities can be better utilized. Furthermore, the scope for pricing and negotiation can be increased, thus enhancing market power.[4]

---

[1] Ct. (Astor, et al., 2016) (Henrich, 2013)
[2] Extracted from (Rothlauf, 2010, p. 33)
[3] Extracted from (Mietzner, 2020)
[4] Ct. (Wirtz, 2006)

# 2 Research questions and reflection

## 2.1 The aim of the work

The aim of this thesis is to examine the transaction environment for medium-sized German companies and to question the motives and obstacles for transactions at medium-sized companies. Derived from this, the reader is to be shown the special features of medium-sized merger and acquisition transactions. In the first part of the thesis, a theoretical basis is formed, which first presents the standard process of such a transaction to the reader.

Subsequently, the results of various studies are analyzed in order to examine the requirements for management consultancies and financiers in more detail.

## 2.2 Structure and methodology

The present work is divided into five chapters. The introduction is followed in this chapter by a description of the objective of the paper, an overview of the basics of M&A and the methodology used in the study. Chapter three then provides the theoretical basis for the following part, chapter four. The final part of the paper, chapter five, serves to present the findings of the investigation.

In order to find out which requirements medium-sized M&A transactions are subject to, a qualitative investigation is carried out. For this purpose, a literature search was carried out to analyze relevant specialist literature and data from current studies were evaluated. The studies used include data collected in surveys conducted among medium-sized companies.

To answer the research question and to include expert opinions and experiences, secondary sources such as statements of M&A consultants and financing in professional journals were also used.

## 2.3    Basics of Mergers & Acquisitions

An analysis of the historical data on the transaction volume per annum shows that the market for mergers and acquisitions is subject to volatility. These fluctuations in transaction volume, which have been considered in some cases in the history of the market and which have been almost wavelike, are known in the literature as the so-called M&A waves.[5] These waves, which appear to be cyclically repeated, lead to an increase and stagnation of transaction volumes in the global mergers & acquisitions market at regularly recurring intervals.[6] It is striking that the emergence of the individual waves is usually accompanied by economic changes, political decisions or technical innovations.[7]

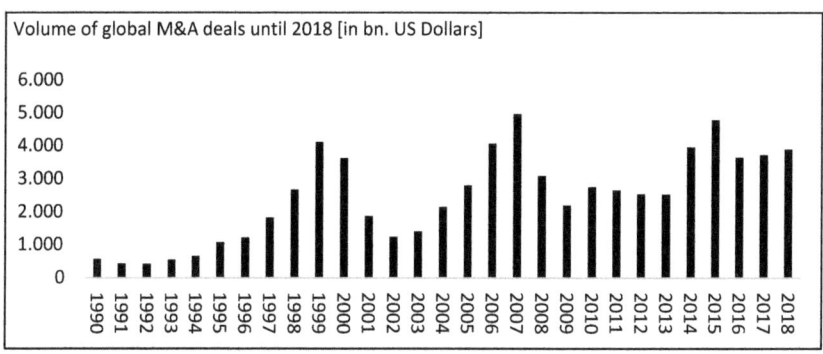

Figure 1: Volume of global M&A deals until 2018 [in bn. US Dollars][8]

Figure 1 shows the cyclical course of M&A waves considering statistical data. The chart clearly shows the wave-like movement of volumes. Especially in the periods 1995 to 2001, 2003 to 2009 and 2013 to 2016.

From the buyer's perspective, M&A transactions are broken down into at least two and up to over ten steps. The subdivision into three phases, a preliminary phase, a transaction phase, and a post-merger/integration phase has become established.[9]

---

[5]Ct. (Schmal, 2016, p. 35) (Ferber, 2013)

[6] Ct. (Institute for Mergers, Acquisitions and Alliances (IMAA), 2019)

[7] Ct. ( Prof. Dr. Theurl, 2007)

[8] Own presentation according to (Institute for Mergers, Acquisitions and Alliances (IMAA), 2019)

[9] Ct. (Dr. Hawranek, 2004, p. 21) (Dr. Fleig, 2019)

Comprehensive strategic planning is required in the preliminary phase, as the processes and concepts developed here for the transaction have a significant impact on the subsequent phases.

A basic strategy is defined in the context of the environment analysis and the corporate goals to be achieved. The SWOT analysis or the use of portfolio concepts can be used as examples. In this way, opportunities and threats from the company's environment can be carefully analyzed and strengths can be identified.[10] From these results, management can decide whether M&A could be useful as a tool for achieving strategic corporate goals.

In the transaction phase, a Letter of Intent (LOI) is drawn up, which documents the letters of intent of both companies to carry out the transaction.[11] Following on from the LOI, in the event of a sale, the M&A advisor carries out an internal due diligence examination of the company to be sold in order to obtain a broader basis of argumentation for the upcoming sales negotiations.

In the area of Due Diligence, the consultant reviews the Financial Due Diligence, the Tax Due Diligence as well as the Environmental Due Diligence. This review forms the basis for assessing the merits of the transaction and for determining the purchase price ranges. During financial due diligence, an auditor or consultant subjects the annual reports such as balance sheet, profit and loss account, and cash flow statement of the target company to a plausibility check. In the subsequent contract negotiations and management discussions, both parties must agree on all takeover modalities and details of the transaction.[12]

Once the fundamental business decisions regarding the takeover have been made, the contract is concluded. This contract defines the business principles, the object of purchase and purchase price including payment modalities as well as the transition date. The transaction phase is concluded with the signing of the contract by the acting managing directors and their notarial certification.[13]

After the successful completion of all requirements of the preliminary phase and the transaction phase, the integration phase follows. The post-merger integration (PMI) applied here is intended to align both companies to work together and generate the desired value-added.[14]

---

[10] (Wietzke, 2019)
[11] Ct. (Nowack, 2017)
[12] Ct. (Dreher & Ernst, 2016)
[13] Ct. (Howson, 2017)
[14] Ct. (Hohnhaus, 2004, p. 65)

# 3 M&A in medium-sized companies

In 2017 there were 3,226,806 companies in Germany.[15] At just under 2.5 million, the vast majority (99.3 %) of companies were small and medium-sized enterprises.[16] According to studies by KfW, Deloitte GmbH, and PricewaterhouseCoopers GmbH, the focus of the M&A market in Germany is clearly on transactions involving family and medium-sized companies. The studies also show that there is a high demand for German companies from global investors.[17] SMEs in the manufacturing sector are particularly popular among non-German investors. Here the share in 2017 was 43% and among German investors 29%.[18]

The motives of the companies are mainly on the sales side of the desired future concentration on the actual core activity of the company. This is to be achieved through the targeted separation of business areas that are no longer subsidized by the selling company or no longer meet the profitability targets of the current shareholders. On the part of the buyers, the desire for additional geographical market development and the realization of cost and scale effects are mentioned as strategic motives. Here the focus is also on achieving sales and cost synergies. The financial background of a Mergers & Acquisitions transaction refers here to the goal of manipulating the financial structure of the company to be acquired. This can be done, for example, by recapitalizing the liabilities side of the balance sheet. In this case, the equity ratio is reduced in favor of the debt capital invested by the buyer.[19]

PricewaterhouseCoopers conducted a survey among medium-sized companies to investigate the purchasing background of past transactions and purchase arguments for future transactions.[20]

---

[15] (Statistisches Bundesamt, 2019)
[16] (Statistisches Bundesamt, 2020)
[17] Ct. (Dr. Müller, 2011) (Dr. Gerstenberger, 2018) (Reker & Götzen, 2012)
[18] (Dr. Gerstenberger, 2018)
[19] Ct (Dreher & Ernst, 2016)
[20] (Dr. Müller, 2011)

As can be seen in Figure 2, the main trigger for transactions was the development of new product markets (60%[21]). In addition to the pressure for efficient company size (23%), this reason is also the driver for future transactions, at 43%.[22]

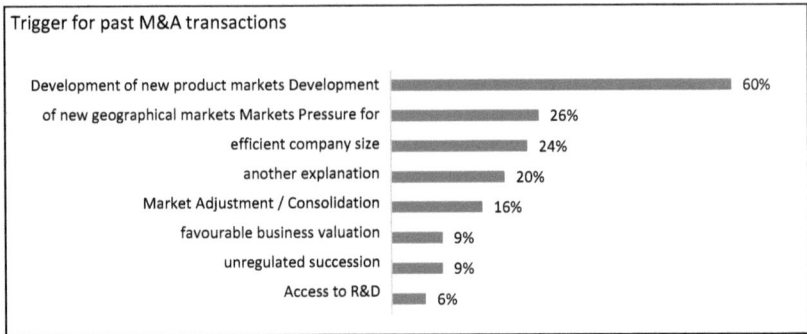

Figure 2: Trigger for past M&A transactions[23]

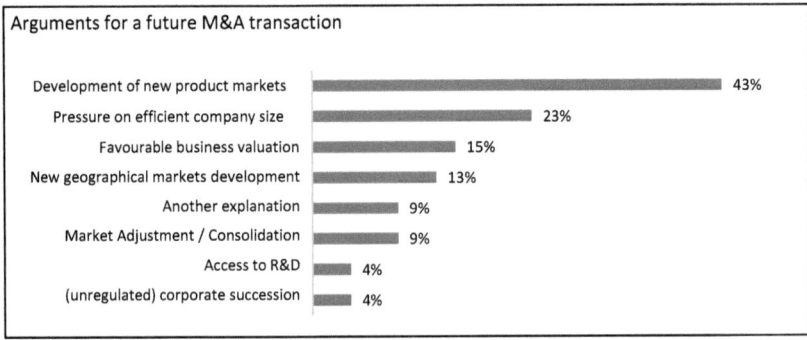

Figure 3: Arguments in favor of M&A transactions[24]

M&A tends to be the exception rather than the rule in SMEs. Statistics show that around 87%[25] of M&A transactions fail in the SME sector. The reasons for this are not only the purchase price but also the complexity of the process and unexpected risks. Therefore, M&A experts and financial service providers advise calling in expert advisors for support.[26]

---

[21] (Dr. Müller, 2011), Basis: All respondents who have carried out a transaction in the past 12 months (n = 55)

[22] (Dr. Müller, 2011), Basis: All respondents who have planned a transaction in the next 12 months (n = 53)

[23] Own presentation according to (Dr. Müller, 2011)

[24] Own presentation according to (Dr. Müller, 2011)

[25] (Reker & Götzen, 2012)

[26] Ct. (Reker & Götzen, 2012) (Wietzke, 2019)

## 3.1 M&A Consulting

Deloitte has conducted a study on the suitability of medium-sized companies with regard to their ownership and corporate structure, strategy, and culture for independently executed M&A transactions. 13% of the respondents see very high suitability of their own company with regard to M&A, 33% estimate the suitability as high and 35% answer with neither. 19% estimate their suitability as low. The survey concluded that M&A transactions tend to be the exception rather than the rule in mid-sized companies. In this respect, expertise, experience and ultimately also the suitability of SMEs with regard to M&A are very heterogeneous.[27]

Often medium-sized companies have excellent managers with detailed functional knowledge, but due to cost pressure, they lack the broad positioning of a group across the entire value chain. This leads to a conflict between operational day-to-day tasks and M&A project support in special projects such as M&A transactions. The "know-how" required in connection with M&A transactions cannot be provided exclusively by the company itself, so consulting services have proven to be a significant help. Especially for small and medium-sized companies, where M&A activities are rare, consultants specialized in M&A activities play a crucial role. In addition to their expertise, they have network relationships within the industry, the banking and the consulting professions.[28]

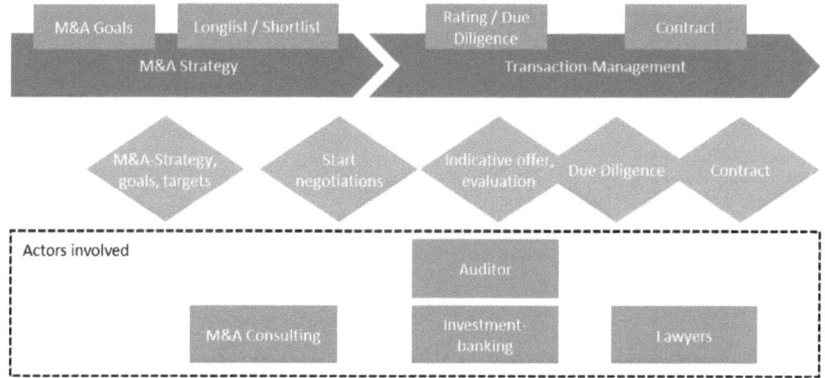

Figure 4: Core competencies, players and project managers in the M&A process[29]

As shown in Figure 4, M&A consultants are involved in the ongoing process of "M&A strategy". The first step is to define the framework for the strategy.

[27] Ct. (Reker & Götzen, 2012)
[28] Ct. (Prof. Dr. Feix, et al., 2017, p. 15 ff.)
[29] Own presentation according to (Prof. Dr. Feix, et al., 2017, p. 28 ff.)

A holistic approach starts with the reflection of the own corporate strategy, which serves as a guideline for the actual objectives and framework. The M&A strategy describes in detail the background of the planned transaction, for example, the development of new markets or the acquisition of new products and services.

The development of the objectives, which should be plausibility checked together with the consultancy and the management, is followed by the preparation of the long list. This list is usually drawn up together with the management and the consultants. The list includes both parties' industry knowledge as well as results of M&A databases such as S&P Capital IQ.[30] Based on predefined evaluation criteria, the longlist is condensed into a shortlist. This includes a selective selection of the most attractive targets from the perspective of derived M&A targets. It is also the starting point for the M&A projects to be pursued.

Based on this list, the identified companies are approached. This is the starting point for negotiations, the first part of which is also supported by consulting. During the ongoing process, the strategy phase passes into the transaction phase, where financial and legal support is required.[31]

---

[30] (S&P Capital IQ, 2020)
[31] Ct. (Prof. Dr. Feix, et al., 2017, p. 15 ff.)

## 3.2    Financial services in M&A

With the beginning of the transaction management from the buyer's point of view, the involve-ment of further actors in the M&A process takes place. These include, as shown in Figure 4 primarily lawyers, bankers and auditors. During this phase, negotiations are conducted, indica-tive offers are analyzed, potential targets are subjected to due diligence and, if successful, pur-chase agreements are finally concluded.[32]

In this context, Deloitte examined the extent of participation of players on the buyer side, which is shown in Figure 3. Lawyers with a rating of 3.0 are involved during the valuations. Bankers with 4.5 and auditors and tax consultants with 4.0. During the subsequent negotiations, lawyers are awarded a 3.4, bankers a 3.0 and auditors and tax consultants a 3.6. The evaluation shows the strong dependence of a company on service providers. In a direct comparison, the managing directors or board members are awarded 3.9 during the valuation phase and 4.3 during negoti-ations. In the evaluation, the high relevance of the financiers, i.e. the banks, stands out.[33]

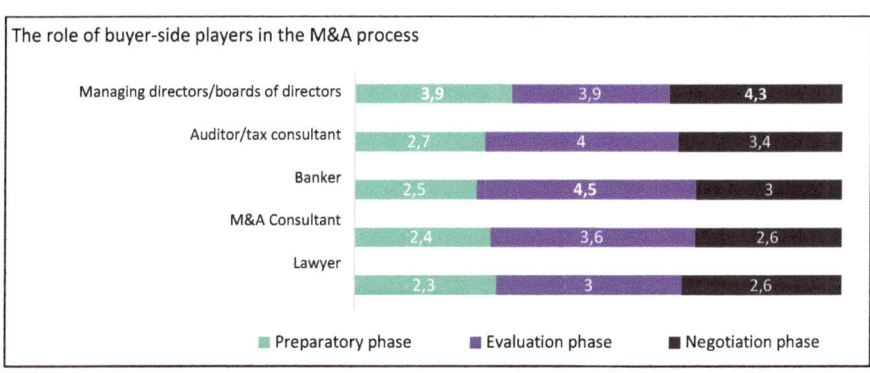

Figure 5 The role of buyer-side players in the M&A process[34]

This can be attributed to the 40 % share of debt capital in financing sources used for M&A trans-actions. Banks play a major role in the financing of company acquisitions. For example, 48% of debt financing is made possible using new bank loans. In 16% of debt financing, companies draw on existing credit lines.[35]

[32] Ct. (Prof. Dr. Feix, et al., 2017, p. 15 ff.)
[33] (Reker & Götzen, 2012, p. 20); Scale: Extent of participation per phase (from 1 = weak to 5 = strong)
[34] Own presentation according to (Reker & Götzen, 2012, p. 20)
[35] (Reker & Götzen, 2012, p. 24)

# 4 M&A requirements of medium-sized companies

From the results, it can be deduced that the expansion of the market position as well as the maintenance of this market position is by far the most important motives for transactions. From this, it can be concluded that in the SME sector it is generally of primary importance to maintain a certain sales area or a certain customer base in order to ensure the continued existence of the company.

Furthermore, it can be concluded that the SME segment plays an extremely important role in advising SMEs before and during the execution of transactions and that SMEs are largely aware of the lack of transaction knowledge in their own company. The required "know-how" can therefore not only be provided by the company itself. External parties such as legal advisors, financiers and auditors are of great importance, especially in the transaction phase. The process-related relevance of the individual parties differs in the two main phases of the transactions. This illustrates the dependence of a successful M&A process on external parties.

With regard to takeover financing, the small and medium-sized company sector is extremely conservative in this respect. The studies show that in 40% of the transactions this segment tries to finance itself in a risk-averse manner via bank loans or existing credit lines.

# 5 Summary and outlook

Especially in times of globalization and the pronounced market entry of competitors from the emerging markets segment, mid-sized companies must view mergers and acquisitions as an opportunity to assert themselves in this changing environment and to maintain or strengthen their competitive position.

As a basis for these transfers, however, advice of all kinds is virtually indispensable. Medium-sized businesses are aware of the problem.

Mergers & Acquisitions are also an absolutely necessary process in the German SME sector, which for strategic reasons must be actively pursued and will become increasingly important in the future. Especially when it comes to defending market shares, it is usually difficult to maintain or expand one's influence, especially in business areas with limited demand. Here, the takeover of a competitor is usually the only possibility for medium-sized companies to expand or diversify.

Against this background, a growing market for advisory services in the area of M&A transactions is also expected. It can, therefore, be assumed that external consulting services, such as M&A advisors, lawyers or auditors as well as financiers, such as banks or private equity companies, will also continue to gain in relevance. In view of the globalization process, these companies should also prepare themselves for cooperation with foreign investors. In addition to legal aspects, this also includes corporate cultural differences and the increasingly interlinked markets.

# List of sources

Prof. Dr. Theurl, T., 2007. *wiwi.uni-muenster.de.* [Online]
Available at: http://www.wiwi.uni-muenster.de/06//studieren/lehrveranstaltungen/2007/material/uki_ws0708_kapitel5+6.pdf
[Accessed 26 12 2019].

Astor, M., Dr. Rammer , C., Klaus, C. & Dr. Klose, G., 2016. *Innovativer Mittelstand 2025 – Herausforderungen, Trends und Handlungsempfehlungen für Wirtschaft und Politik,* Berlin: Bundesministeriums für Wirtschaft und Energie.

Dr. Fleig, J., 2019. *business-wissen.de.* [Online]
Available at: https://www.business-wissen.de/artikel/ma-das-phasenmodell-einer-ma-transaktion/
[Accessed 26 12 2019].

Dr. Gerstenberger, J., 2018. *M&A-Deals im deutschen Mittelstand –Verarbeitendes Gewerbe besonders gefragt,* Frankfurt am Main: KfW Research.

Dr. Hawranek, F., 2004. *Schnittstellenmanagement bei M&A-Transaktionen.* Wiesbaden: Deutscher Universitätsverlag.

Dr. Müller, C., 2011. *Transaktionen im Mittelstand – Bestandsaufnahme und Ausblick,* Frankfurt am Main: PricewaterhouseCoopers AG Wirtschaftsprüfungsgesellschaft.

Dreher, M. & Ernst, D., 2016. *Mergers & Acquisitions: Grundlagen und Verkaufsprozess mittlerer und großer Unternehmen.* München: Uni-Taschenbücher.

Ferber, M., 2013. Kein Übernahmefieber trotz Aktien-Hausse. *Neue Züricher Zeitung.*

Henrich, A., 2013. *wiwo.de*. [Online]
Available at: https://www.wiwo.de/unternehmen/mittelstand/wachsende-konkurrenz-was-jetzt-zu-tun-ist/8998546-2.html
[Accessed 02 02 2020].

Hohnhaus, W., 2004. *Erfolg der M&A-Beratung bei Unternehmenstransaktionen*. Wiesbaden: Deutscher Universitätsverlag.

Howson, P., 2017. *Due diligence: The critical stage in mergers and acquisitions*. London: Taylor & Francis Group.

Institute for Mergers, Acquisitions and Alliances (IMAA), 2019. *statista.com*. [Online]
Available at: https://de.statista.com/statistik/daten/studie/153735/umfrage/volumen-der-fusionen-und-uebernahmen-weltweit/
[Accessed 26 12 2019].

Mietzner, J.-P. D. M., 2020. *wirtschaftslexikon.gabler.de*. [Online]
Available at: https://wirtschaftslexikon.gabler.de/definition/mergers-acquisitions-41789
[Accessed 02 02 2020].

Nowack, S., 2017. *psp.eu*. [Online]
Available at: https://www.psp.eu/artikel/308/der-letter-of-intent-im-rahmen-von-unternehmenstransaktionen/
[Accessed 26 12 2019].

Prof. Dr. Feix, T., Prof. Dr. Büchler, J.-P. & Prof. Dr. Straub, T., 2017. *Mergers & Acquisitions: Erfolgsfaktoren für mittelständische Unternehmen*. Freiburg: Haufe-Lexware GmbH & Co. KG.

Reker, J. & Götzen, S., 2012. *Mergers & Acquisitions im Mittelstand,* Bamberg: Deloitte Mittelstandsinstitut.

Rothlauf, J., 2010. *Total Quality Management in Theorie und Praxis: Zum ganzheitlichen Unternehmensverständnis.* Oldenbourg: De Gruyter Oldenbourg.

S&P Capital IQ, 2020. *spglobal.com.* [Online]
Available at: https://www.spglobal.com/marketintelligence/en/solutions/transactions
[Accessed 17 1 2020].

Schmal, S., 2016. *Konsolidierungs- und M&A-Wellen.* Oldenburg: Universität Oldenburg.

Statistisches Bundesamt, 2019. *destatis.de.* [Online]
Available at:
https://www.destatis.de/DE/Themen/Staat/Steuern/Umsatzsteuer/Publikationen/Downloads-Umsatzsteuern/umsatzsteuer-2140810177004.pdf?__blob=publicationFile&v=2
[Accessed 7 1 2020].

Statistisches Bundesamt, 2020. *destatis.de.* [Online]
Available at: https://www.destatis.de/DE/Themen/Branchen-Unternehmen/Unternehmen/Kleine-Unternehmen-Mittlere-Unternehmen/_inhalt.html
[Accessed 6 1 2020].

Wietzke, S. P. W., 2018. *ifwniggemann.de.* [Online]
Available at: https://ifwniggemann.de/wordpress/wp-content/uploads/2017/12/Wachstum-durch-MA-von-der-Strategie-zum-Erwerb-Wietzke.pdf
[Accessed 9 1 2019].

Wietzke, S. P. W., 2019. *ifwniggemann.de.* [Online]
Available at: https://ifwniggemann.de/wordpress/wp-content/uploads/2017/12/Wachstum-durch-MA-von-der-Strategie-zum-Erwerb-Wietzke.pdf
[Accessed 26 12 2019].

Wirtz, B. W., 2006. *ibu.kit.edu.* [Online]

Available at: https://www.ibu.kit.edu/rd_download/SVZ_-_07_-
_Ziele_Unternehmenszusammenschluesse.pdf

[Accessed 02 02 2020].

| Subject area | |
|---|---|
| Economics | In the field of economics, the aim is to investigate how the market reacts to an M&A transaction. Possibly, M&A strategies can be improved by investigating competitors. In addition, customers will be asked how they perceive a possible transaction.<br><br>In the field of media, it has to be investigated whether the M&A transaction could lead to negative publications. |
| Marketing & Communication | In the area of marketing and communication, it must be investigated how a possible M&A transaction could influence existing customer relationships. In addition, it must be investigated which new markets can be developed. |
| HR & Leadership Competencies | In the area of HR & Leadership Competencies, a PMI must examine how strongly cultural differences could influence the transaction and how a successful PMI should be conducted. |
| Corporate Finance | M&A transactions are a part of Corporate Finance and therefore firmly anchored in this field.<br><br>In the area of corporate financing, it must be decided what financial resources will be used for the transaction and how much budget can ultimately be made available. The danger of too much investment, which later ties up too many financial resources in the M&A process, should, therefore, be avoided. It should be examined how the merger or acquisition can support the primary goal of increasing the value of the company and increase the return on investment without exceeding the company's own risk-bearing capacity. |
| Strategic Corporate Management | Strategic management is the branch of business administration that deals with the development, planning, and implementation of content-related goals and orientations of organizations. For this |

| | |
|---|---|
| | purpose, it is, therefore, necessary to examine how an M&A transaction can be incorporated into the long-term implementation of the company's objectives. |
| International Business Law | For international transactions, it is necessary to examine the legal situation. These may concern labor law and patent rights. In addition, the purchase agreements must be adapted to the local conditions. |
| Value-Based Controlling & Int. Accounting | In Value Based Management (VBM), the management philosophy and management approach that enables and supports maximum value creation in organizations is usually the maximization of shareholder value. VBM encompasses the processes for creating, managing and measuring value. In this sense, it is important to consider how cost structures in the company change as a result of an M&A transaction. This may involve new transfer prices or cost reductions, for example. |
| Research Methods | In the area of research, it is necessary to investigate which databases are suitable for the target industry and how they should be used. |

# YOUR KNOWLEDGE HAS VALUE

- We will publish your bachelor's and
  master's thesis, essays and papers

- Your own eBook and book -
  sold worldwide in all relevant shops

- Earn money with each sale

Upload your text at www.GRIN.com
and publish for free